Famous Explorers™

Ferdinand Magellan

Claude Hurwicz

The Rosen Publishing Group's
PowerKids Press™
New York

To Amy and Gregory Hurwicz

Published in 2001 by The Rosen Publishing Group, Inc.
29 East 21st Street, New York, NY 10010

Photo Credits: Cover and title page, pp. 4, 11 (King Charles I), 16, 20 © North Wind Pictures; p. 2 © Art Resource; pp. 2, 3, 8, 12, 19 © The Granger Collection, New York; pp. 2, 3, 9, 15 © SuperStock; p. 7 © A.K.G. Berlin/SuperStock; p. 11 (King Manuel I) © CORBIS.

First Edition

Book Design: Maria Melendez and Felicity Erwin

Hurwicz, Claude.
  Ferdinand Magellan / by Claude Hurwicz.
       p. cm. — (Famous explorers)
  Summary: Describes the life and travels of the Portuguese sea captain who commanded the first expedition that sailed around the world.
ISBN 0-8239-5562-1 (lib. bdg.)
  1. Magalhães., Fernão de, d.1521–Juvenile literature. 2. Explorers—Portugal—Biography–Juvenile literature. 3. Voyages around the world–Juvenile literature. [1. Magellan, Ferdinand, d. 1521. 2. Explorers. 3. Voyages around the world.] I. Title. II. Series.

G420.M2 H87 2000
910.4'1—dc21
[B]   99-049976

Contents

4

Trained to Explore

Ferdinand Magellan was born in Portugal around 1480. Magellan lived during the Age of Exploration, which lasted from the 1400s to the 1800s. During this time, the rulers of Europe sent explorers to claim land and bring back riches. These explorers traveled to India and Asia, and to what we now call North, South, and Central America.

In the 1400s, boys who were related to the royal family could work and get an education at the king's **court**. Magellan was related to King John II of Portugal. He went to the royal courts to work as a **page** and to study **astronomy**, mapmaking, and **navigation**.

In this picture, Magellan is holding a sextant. A sextant measures the angle of stars and planets to figure out which way a ship is headed.

Riches and Adventure

At King John II's court, Magellan heard about the adventures of many explorers. The explorers came back with goods from Asia and India. They brought back **spices**, fine cloth, and **gems**. These goods could not be found in Europe. Europeans who wanted these goods had to pay a lot of money for them. Magellan knew that he could make money and see new places if he became an explorer.

In 1505, Magellan made his first sea journey. He joined some **traders** sailing east from Portugal. They sailed up the east coast of Africa. Their ship reached India in 1507. Magellan spent the next seven years working for trading **expeditions**.

Magellan and other traders brought back goods from India and Asia. This picture shows the port in Lisbon, Portugal.

7

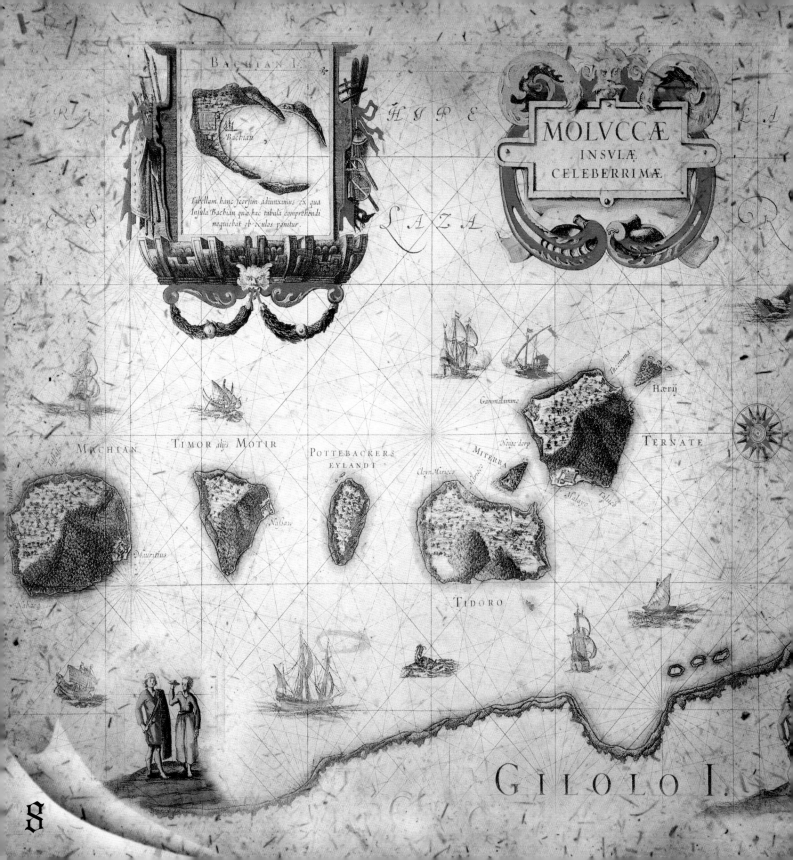

BACHIAN I.

Bachian

Tabellam hanc seorsim adiunximus ex qua
Insula Bachian quæ hac tabula comprehendi
nequibat ob oculos ponitur.

HIPE

LAZA

MOLVCCÆ
INSVLÆ
CELEBERRIMÆ

Grammalamme

Th. onma

Hærij

MITERRA

Sjoge dorp

TERNATE

MACHIAN

TIMOR alijs MOTIR

POTTEBACKERS
EYLANDT

Cleyn Marieca

Malavo Taluca

Nassaw

Mauritius

TIDORO

Nabaru

GILOLO I.

8

The Spice Islands

As a trader Magellan traveled to the Spice Islands. These islands were named for the **valuable** spices that grew there.

Indian spices.

It took months for European traders to get to the Spice Islands. The seas were very rough and the islands were far away. Traders wanted to find shorter ways to get there from Europe. Until the early 1500s, they had reached the Spice Islands by traveling east. Magellan thought it would be faster to travel west. He also thought there was a passageway in South America that led from the Atlantic to the Pacific Ocean. People did not know how big the Pacific Ocean was. No one had ever crossed it. Magellan thought that crossing the Pacific would be a short trip.

An engraved map of the Spice Islands. The map comes from an atlas made in 1662.

Sailing for the Spanish King

Magellan wanted to try his new route to the Spice Islands. He went to King Manuel I, the new king of Portugal, to ask for money for the journey. King Manuel I did not like Magellan and would not give him the money he needed.

In 1517, Magellan went to see King Charles I of Spain to ask for help. There was an agreement between Spain and Portugal saying that all land east of a certain point belonged to Portugal. The agreement also said that all land west of that point belonged to Spain. If Magellan reached the Spice Islands by sailing west, then the Spice Islands would belong to Spain. King Charles I wanted control of the Spice Islands. He gave Magellan money for his voyage.

King Charles I of Spain gave Magellan money for his journey. Magellan promised to claim the Spice Islands for Spain.

King Manuel I
of Portugal

Europe

Portugal

Spain

King Charles I
of Spain

11

Preparing for the Journey

Magellan bought five ships for his journey west to the Spice Islands. The names of these ships were *San Antonio*, *Trinidad*, *Victoria*, *Concepcion*, and *Santiago*. It was hard for Magellan to find men to sail with him. The journey was dangerous and he could not pay much money. He traveled around Europe to find sailors.

Magellan also had to get supplies. He bought biscuits, salted beef, and pork. He bought lanterns to light the ship. He also bought weapons and gunpowder for the crew of about 241 men. Magellan brought goods to trade for spices. He brought copper bracelets, colored bells, and knives.

An Italian named Antonio Pigafetta sailed with Magellan. He kept a diary of the voyage. Pigafetta was one of the few men to survive. Much of what we know about the journey comes from his description.

Magellan could only afford to buy old ships. He had to repair them before leaving for the Spice Islands.

13

South America

In 1519, Magellan sailed from Spain. The crew traveled across the Atlantic Ocean for three months. They landed on the coast of South America, in the country now called Brazil.

Brazil belonged to Portugal. Magellan was sailing for Spain, Portugal's enemy. He thought the Portuguese would attack if the sailors stayed in Brazil. They rested for a short time, and then left Brazil.

Magellan continued down the coast of South America. He thought that he was close to the **strait**, or passageway, between the Atlantic and Pacific Oceans. The weather was freezing cold and the sea was rough. The crew was tired and wanted to go home.

In Brazil, Magellan and his men saw monkeys and parrots, animals they had never seen before.

South America

Brazil

Portugal

Spain

Europe

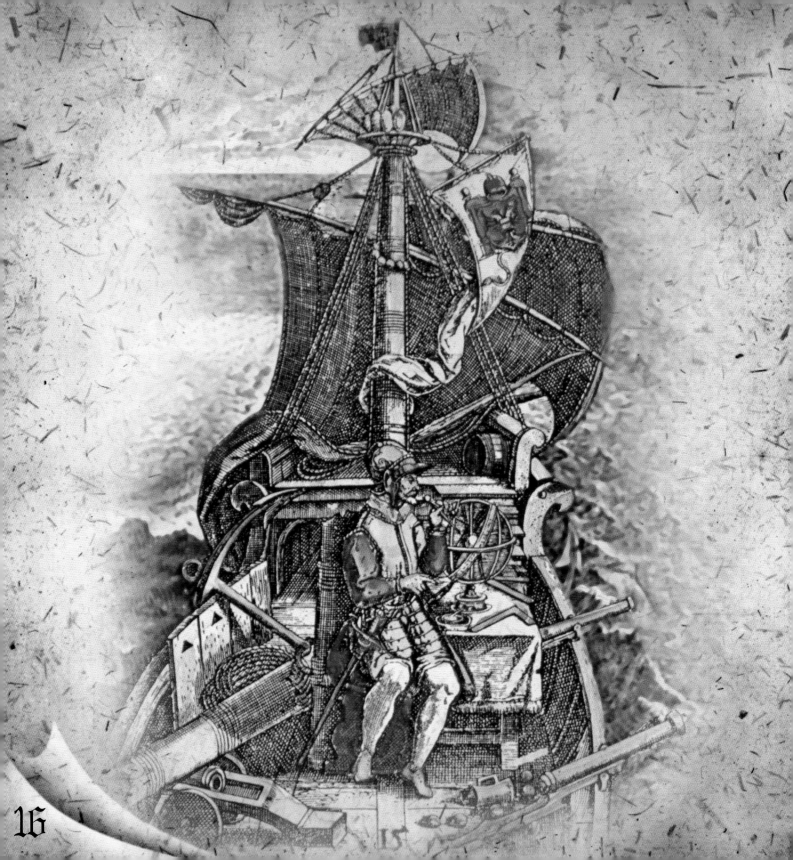

The Straits of Magellan

Four months after leaving Spain, Magellan still had not found a passageway from the Atlantic Ocean to the Pacific Ocean. In the winter of 1519, some of Magellan's men tried to take control of the expedition. Magellan killed some of the men who **rebelled**. He left two men in South America with no food or water. Magellan wanted to warn his men that they should not try to take control away from him again.

In October of 1520, Magellan finally found the passageway that led to the Pacific Ocean. The strait was at the southern end of South America. Later it was named the Straits of Magellan.

Stories say that the sailors saw giants in South America. These "giants" were probably Indian men who were taller than European men and dressed in animal skins instead of clothes.

By the time Magellan reached the strait, one ship had sunk and another had headed back to Spain.

17

Crossing the Pacific

agellan had found the waterway that connected the Atlantic and Pacific Oceans. He thought he would get to the Spice Islands in a few more days.

In fact, it took over 30 days to pass through the waterway that is now known as the Straits of Magellan. In November of 1520, Magellan and his men finally reached the Pacific Ocean. Six weeks later they had not seen land. The crew ran out of food. They had to eat sawdust, leather straps, and even rats. Many men starved to death.

The Pacific Ocean was much bigger than Magellan had thought. It took almost four months to cross.

The crew had no food. This caused a lot of them to get sick with scurvy, a disease that develops when you don't get enough fruits and vegetables. Scurvy makes your bones ache, your gums bleed, and your teeth fall out.

This picture shows Magellan and his men reaching the Pacific Ocean after passing through the strait.

Victoria

Death in the Philippines

On March 28, 1521, Magellan docked near a group of islands called the Philippines. The people in the Philippines, called Filipinos, spoke a language like the language spoken in the Spice Islands. People who live near each other often speak a **similar** language. Since the Filipinos understood the language of the Spice **Islanders**, Magellan thought he was near these islands.

Magellan got along with most of the people who lived in the Philippines. The leader on the island of Mactan did not like Magellan though, because Magellan was friendly with the Mactans' enemies. The Mactans and Magellan's crew had a battle. Magellan was hit with a poisoned arrow and stabbed. He died on April 27, 1521.

Magellan traded peacefully with many Filipinos. The Mactans did not like him though, and killed him in a battle in 1521.

Heading Home Without Magellan

After Magellan's death, the crew continued the journey. They reached the Spice Islands and bought a spice called clove at a cheap price. Then they sailed home.

In September 1522, the ship *Victoria* reached Spain. Only 18 of the 241 men made it back alive.

Ferdinand Magellan was one of the greatest explorers of all time. He did not live to finish his journey, but he is known as the first man to **circumnavigate**, or sail all the way around, the world.

Magellan's Timeline

1519-Magellan begins his journey to the Spice Islands.

1520-Magellan reaches the Pacific Ocean.

1521-Magellan is killed in the Philippines.

1522-Magellan's crew returns to Spain.

Glossary

astronomy (uh-STRON-oh-mee) The study of the sun, moon, planets, and stars.

circumnavigate (SER-kem-NA-vuh-gayt) To sail all the way around.

court (KORT) Where a king or queen lives.

expeditions (EX-spuh-DISH-unz) Trips taken for a special purpose.

gems (JEMZ) Jewels.

islanders (EYE-lan-durz) People who live on an island.

navigation (NA-vuh-GAY-shun) A way of figuring out which way a ship is headed.

page (PAYJ) A young man studying at the palace of a king or queen.

rebelled (ruh-BELD) When someone has disobeyed the people in charge.

similar (SIM-uh-ler) Almost the same as.

spices (SPY-sez) A seasoning that adds flavor to food.

strait (STRAYT) A passageway between two bodies of water.

traders (TRAY-derz) People who buy and sell things.

valuable (VAL-yoo-uh-buhl) Worth a lot of money.

Index

Web Sites

To learn more about Ferdinand Magellan, check out these Web sites:

http://www.mariner.org/age/magellan.html

http://www.skittler.demon.co.uk/magellan.htm